Wanderlust:

For the Young, Broke Professional

Because traveling
should not just be a luxury for the rich

DEIDRE N. MATHIS

authorHOUSE®

AuthorHouse™
1663 Liberty Drive
Bloomington, IN 47403
www.authorhouse.com
Phone: 1-800-839-8640

Published by AuthorHouse 01/09/2015

ISBN: 978-1-4969-6252-2 (sc)
ISBN: 978-1-4969-6251-5 (e)

Library of Congress Control Number: 2015900352

Thank you to all of my great friends and family who encouraged me to write this book and have supported me throughout it all.

Thank you to all of the strangers I met in other places of the world who are now no longer strangers at all-but now some of my closest friends.

To the people who have emailed, texted and called me to tell me I had inspired them to step outside of their comfort zones and travel the world - YOU are the real rock star!

Contents

What is a Young, Broke Professional?

Let me start by welcoming you to the first page in a new chapter of your life: a chapter where you embrace the best and least predictable adventure that life has to offer – travel.

This is no ordinary travel book. It focuses closely on the needs of the YBP, or Young Broke Professional, largely based on my own experiences.

I'm Deidre Mathis, and for a long time, I have had a serious case of *wanderlust*. I have traveled to some of the most beautiful and exotic locations in the world, including India, Puerto Rico, South Africa, Hawaii, Mexico, and many more destinations within and beyond the U.S.A. In fact, I've traveled to over 23 countries in the past few years and my life has been far, far better for it. Thanks to travel, it has been extraordinary.

Am I a millionaire? Not yet! Do I have some mysterious circumstances that mean I have to hop on a plane every few weeks? No! I am simply, like you, a Young Broke Professional, who has a genuine passion for exploring the world we are all lucky enough to live in.

So – how can we define a Young Broke Professional? While I believe in the saying: "you are only as young as you feel," the typical YBP is normally between the ages of 18 and 35. You could be in almost any situation: in college, recently graduated, or thinking of taking a break in the middle of your career. Naturally, as a young person, you are more than likely still building up to a peak of professional and financial security. In other words, while you could be looking forward to the comfort money can bring in your later years, you are now yearning to use the skills you have acquired thus far to travel and explore the world, although you may not have a ton of cash set away to do so.

But…

You are a YBP who wants to experience the best the world has to offer, *the world* itself. You, like me, want to see the Taj Mahal, one of the New 7 Wonders of the World, from just a few feet away. You, like me, might like to try Mofongo, a delicious plantain-based Puerto Rican delicacy, just because it has a cool name. And you, just like me, get a real thrill from landing somewhere new, knowing you can meet the locals, absorb all the sights and simply… explore.

A YBP with a true case of wanderlust refuses to sit at home wishing he or she had more money to travel the world in style. They simply pick up this book and get going!

It's great to be a YBP! Who needs stacks of dollars, when with a little planning and a spirit of adventure, you can visit the best places in the world in a manner that suits your budget? Even without much money, the world can still be your oyster – *Wanderlust* will show you how.

It is important to indulge any feelings of wanderlust that you may be experiencing as a YBP. Why? Well, first of all, travel is as good as it gets. Yes, you can spend the money you have by simply collecting 'stuff' – clothes, gadgets, cars – but what is it that you will look back on when you are old and gray? Not a designer T-shirt, but your happiest memories, and travel will provide a ton of those.

Second, as a YBP you probably have a rewarding life ahead of you, including success in your career, family life, and the responsibility that comes with all that. For now though, you are young and free to travel if you wish. No one ever regrets visiting too many countries, having too much uplifting fun, seeing too many stunning views, tasting too much amazing new food, or swimming at the foot of too many cascading waterfalls…quite the opposite. As I urge you toward the end of this book, it is simply a case of living your life according to the Latin motto *carpe diem*, or 'seize the day.'

There really is no time like the present. After all, you have been getting feelings of wanderlust for a reason. Think about your own reasons for wanting to travel. Is it because you feel that you have not seen much outside of your own home town and wish to spread your wings? Are you chasing some sun-kissed days spent on palm-fringed white beaches? Do you want to learn a new language in its country of origin? Are you excited to mix with people from wildly different cultures? Are you yearning for a great big taste of exotic foods, drink and music? Do you love the idea of getting close to nature in far-flung locations? Or do you simply long to see the some of the best places in the world, wherever they may be?

It is entirely possible that all of the reasons above (and possibly more) inspire you to travel. It will be my pleasure to help you make that particular dream come true.

In fact, getting away is not rocket science. We all sometimes think of the obstacles to achieving what we want as being insurmountable. Have you ever thought to yourself:

"I can't travel because I just haven't got enough money / time / travel companions / knowledge / courage to explore the world?"

Well, don't panic. Everyone can feel that way, even the most resourceful and strongest-willed YBPs. We address each of these perceived obstacles in *Wanderlust* and look at the many ways to get you on that plane and off into the world. This book is an essential resource that, along with your passport, will hand you the world on a plate.

I sincerely hope you enjoy *Wanderlust* as the book that will help get your travel dreams off the ground. Now, get busy reading- soon you'll be busy packing!

Bon voyage,

Deidre Mathis

Tick, Tock - Time to Get Away

Exciting isn't it? As you read through this book you will go on a unique journey – perhaps even the very first of many – as you discover how you can enjoy experiencing more travel.

Every journey starts with a departure, of course, but even before that it starts in the mind. It could be the mental image you are cherishing of lush Amazon rainforest from a TV program you saw last week, or it could be a desire to visit a buzzing city that has captured your imagination for years, like Tokyo or Barcelona.

I don't have to tell you how to dream – every YBP knows that already. But what I can do is give practical, helpful advice, based on my own experiences, to get you on the right road.

First stop: make some plans…

It's All in the Planning

Shouldn't travel be a carefree experience where you make your way from one gorgeous new place to another - a sort of voyage of discovery?

Well it certainly can be that, but to ensure that you have the best possible time when you do go away, you first need to plan in advance.

It's never too early to start planning. Begin, of course, with the destination itself, as it will dictate certain things about your trip. For example, let's say you are longing to go to Jamaica to soak up some Caribbean sun. Take a look online and you will discover that the high season is from roughly mid-December through mid-April. You would be right to infer that the hottest, driest weather will be during this time. However, as a YBP you would also be right to assume that some accommodations and flight deals may be less expensive out of the peak season. If you go off-peak, you may experience some wet weather – but then again, you may just be the sort of person who would prefer to save some money, and would love to dance barefoot on a beach in the midst of a warm shower of rain...

Next, think about some must-sees while you are there. Have fun, search online for activity suggestions in your destination, and start picturing yourself there. Read up on other travelers' reviews of locations and for inspiration. Let your mind wander about where you want to go and what you want to do. This is a really enjoyable part of planning any trip.

If you are thinking of going to India, for example, you may also be very excited about cramming in as many opportunities as possible to experience the vibrant culture, architecture, delicious food, dazzlingly beautiful natural scenery, and loud, busy, cities. When I thought about it, I realized that I needed a good amount of time in-country to create the trip I wanted, so I planned to stay there for seven weeks. I lived in Jaipur, the bustling capital of Rajasthan, which is also known as 'Pink City' due to the rose-colored buildings in the city.

Plan:

- Pick a country (or *countries*) you plan to travel to soon.
- Research online to determine the best seasons to travel for weather, festivals, etc.
- Choose the must-see towns, monuments, and scenery.
- Add in your must-do activities, like a safari, a trip to meet local charity workers, or a bungee jump.
- Plan out how much time you think may wish to spend in your destination(s) at this stage.

Now that you have a rough outline of your trip, you can begin considering other practicalities you'll need to sort out before you set off!

Prioritize Your Life

If you are genuinely going to indulge your appetite for travel, you are going to have to decide to prioritize travel in your life.

This is exactly what I have done.

Traveling is NOT just a hobby for me, it's my lifestyle. I save money to travel, I work for travel, I live to travel.

Of course, family and friends come first. If you have loved ones in circumstances that restrict you from traveling right away, that is a valid reason (but you can still plan for when that situation changes). Otherwise, most obstacles can be overcome.

"Oh yeah?" I can hear you saying to yourself, *"it's not that easy, Deidre."*
But it is absolutely true. Let's say you've been in your ideal job for the past year and do not want to risk losing it by traveling. Have you considered talking to your boss about your desire to travel in a positive and constructive way? You may be able to use existing holiday allowance, or even take extended unpaid leave. You could work with the management to choose travel dates which coincide with their least busy times. You many even select a location where it would be useful to your company to have you stay there for a few weeks. Who knows? Every working situation is different, but one thing is for sure – if you don't ask, you won't receive.

Once you have gotten your head around the time off question, you need to think about its ugly cousin, the money factor. The trick with money is never to panic. This is *your* trip. It can be done as cheaply as you can manage, if you wish. Or, it can be shorter and more indulgent. Prioritize what is important to you. If you want to soak up the local culture, forget the touristy hotels and look into cheaper options like home stays. Find out if you might have a friend of a friend living out in the country. We cover all this in the Accommodations section, but the point is – you have many choices.

Saving makes sense. Work out how long you're going to travel and how much you can realistically save. It is always good to travel with emergency cash sitting in your bank, not to be touched. You probably won't use it, but it is very reassuring.

Plus, for longer trips, and depending on how long you are planning to stay, nothing is stopping you from doing some paid work in your chosen destination. If you are looking at several months' travel, you'd be crazy not to consider how you could supplement your income in a fun, rewarding way, such as teaching English, or for you night owls, working in a bar. Not everything has to go on your official résumé once you get back home (although a little bit of interesting travel always looks good)!

We will go into the money aspect in more detail later in the book. In the meantime, here are a few valuable tips regarding another valuable resource – time:

Five Tips for Making Time to Travel

1. Be brave – There is nothing like prioritizing your travel plans to find out suddenly that other problems just seem to melt away. So you had been thinking about attending that music concert in March, but you find an incredibly good deal to visit China at the same time - it's all about priorities. Do you snag the good trip or postpone it yet again?
2. Get organized – Look at what priorities need to be taken care of during the week, month, or year that you will be away traveling. Figure out what is urgent and important, important but not urgent,

and what is not important in your personal and professional life.

Divide up all of your tasks into these categories then complete, delegate, or eliminate all the items you can; you might be surprised at how few things MUST be done in the time you are away. When it comes to most jobs, none of us are truly indispensable (for a little while anyway).

3. Bargain with colleagues – Take on extra work and responsibility for them now – manage that project you had been ignoring, or lead some meetings – in return for them picking up the slack while you are away. Fair deal.

4. Get family on your side – It is not just work that demands a lot of your time. Our loved ones can, in the nicest possible way, require a lot of time and effort. If you have a particularly close or high maintenance family network, you may feel unable to travel for long periods. *They might worry!* Take it from me: if you explain yourself well and tell them how much the trip means to you and show them how well-prepared you are; they are bound to support you. If not, you can still send them a lovely postcard!

5. Make good use of long weekends- If you have a day off on a Friday, leave for your trip Thursday night and come back Sunday evening. This has instantly given you a four day, three night trip.

For trips that are quite a distance away, take off a week of work (five days) and turn that into a 10 day, nine night trip, instantly. Example: If you take off a week of work in

April 2015 from April 6th- 10th, you can leave for your trip on the evening on Friday, April 3rd and return on the eve of Sunday, April 12th, and you have made great use of just a week of vacation days.

Now you are starting to get a good idea of the commitment required to ensure that you have enough time, money, and resources to devote to your travel plans. It doesn't have to be very hard work. Your imagination and determination is the key to unlocking the wonderful potential of that passport.

Sorting the Paperwork

Of course, no one's going on any international trip without the right paperwork. Everyone needs a passport, and in some cases, a visa too. Here's the lowdown on getting organized. My passport is my favorite document – we have shared some great adventures together. A passport quite simply opens up the world to you. Plus, all of your stamped pages make for a remarkable keepsake.

Obtaining Essential Travel Documents

No passport yet? No problem! You just need to get one, as soon as possible.
Here's how in a few simple steps:

    a. Go to US Passports and International Travel website, or this link:

http://travel.state.gov/content/passports/english/passports/apply.html

    b. Work your way through the online guide to confirm eligibility. Be prepared to provide information like your date of birth. Check passport book as the document of choice (cost is $110) and note that it could take up to six weeks for your passport to be processed unless you choose the faster, Expedited

Processing service which currently costs $60 and take 2-3 weeks. You can also choose delivery options.

TIP – Apply as early as possible and save yourself money.

c. You will apply for your actual passport at a Passport Agency or other authorized facility. They will ask you for certain documents:
   1. An original document as evidence of U.S. citizenship (which will be returned to you after your application is processed.) The online guide lists which documents may be used, such as a U.S. Birth Certificate or previous U.S. passport.
   2. Photo identification, like a driver's license.
   3. A photocopy of that identification.

d. Go to a photo booth and take a color, 2 x 2 inch photo. Your face must not be obscured – refer to the guide for full details.
e. You will also need a form DS-11, which has been completed but not signed. You can download a DS-11 form online, from the same guide (link above).
f. Go to your nearest Passport Acceptance Facility – there is a handy online search page at this address: http://iafdb.travel.state.gov/

Just sign the form in front of the authorized person, pay your dues, and then sit back and wait for your passport to freedom!

Visas

This one's really easy. As you know, a visa is like an official pass that you need to go to certain countries. Each country has its own visa rules, so general advice will not be helpful here. All you have to do is go to this website:

US Visas, Americans Traveling Abroad -

http://travel.state.gov/content/visas/english/general/americans-traveling-abroad.html

Here, you will find all the vital country-specific information that you need. Select your destination from the drop-down menu and follow all the latest advice closely. Typically, you will have to obtain a visa from the embassy of the country you want to visit. Allow plenty of time to apply for this process, as it can take several weeks. However, depending on where you are going, you might not even need a visa!

TIP – On this same webpage you will not only find out about visa and exit requirements, you will also have all the latest safety updates, plus – DO read and take whatever advice is give about vaccinations.

Vaccinations

Being ill abroad is an experience that can frequently be avoided if you take sensible precautions.

One major precaution that is always advised is having the vaccinations that are stated on the US Travel website above:

http://travel.state.gov/content/visas/english/general/ americans-traveling-abroad.html

You will find country-specific details about the vaccinations you will need to have before visiting a certain country. Do not mess around with this advice – it is vital. If you need to, make an appointment with a doctor and get your vaccinations sorted out, as you don't want to come home with any nasty souvenirs.

Also, you should note that some vaccinations are not necessarily optional. In some circumstances you will need to show proof that you have been vaccinated before you can enter the country. For example the advice for Nigeria currently reads:

"A yellow fever vaccination certificate is required for travelers over one year of age arriving within six days from infected areas."
Stay informed about the latest vaccination enquiries online and while you are at it, it makes sense to read about the wider health advice being offered by the authorities.

Your Safety Net – The Lowdown on Travel Insurance

No one likes to think of things going wrong when they travel abroad. On the other hand, everyone likes the idea of a safety net that gives you peace of mind. When you travel, don't skip the travel insurance. It's not just an extra expense: if you are going to somewhere with moderate risk, or want to participate in water sports or other activities…even if you just want a regular trip, you need to think about travel insurance.

Choosing the right policy could be the difference between making sure you get a helicopter transfer to hospital if you break a leg while climbing up a mountain in Bueno Aires, or are covered for stolen luggage in Ireland. It could save your trip, or even save your life.

Travel insurance can be relatively cheap or very expensive, depending on a wide range of factors, including your destination, the state of your health, the length of your stay, and so on. So, how can you get a real bargain?

My recommendation is to visit the travel insurance comparison website that has received ample praise and awards for being a reliable resource:

www.squaremouth.com

Take a look, fill in your details, and see exactly what policies are offered for your trip. All the insurance agencies are rated, which is helpful. Select the best one, pay up, and you're good to go!

TIP – Tempting though it may be, don't simply choose the cheapest policy without thinking it through. Do read the small print and know exactly what you are covered for before you buy.

A to Z of Accommodations

One of the many great things about travel is that you get to choose your ideal home for the days or weeks to come. If you have always wanted to live in a beach shack, you can try it. If you want to enjoy the most luxurious rooms your budget will stretch to, nothing's stopping you.

So, what will it be?

Hotel, hostel, or home stay?

Each country has its own unique configuration of accommodations, and they may vary hugely from area to area. For example, in the Caribbean, you many find many large tourist-friendly hotels dominating most of the major beaches, but nearby, if you look, you are also likely to find options for staying in more modest and affordable accommodations.

Here's a look at the pros and cons of various types of accommodations.

Hotels

Hotels can provide you a huge variety of styles. The typical hotel offers a reliable welcome for the traveler, with relative safety and comfort. Many will offer superior meals and clean water in remote or inhospitable locations. They may offer first-rate facilities, like swimming pools and air-conditioned bedrooms. Some will offer the chance to communicate with the outside world through telephone and the internet. On the whole, hotel staff members are friendly and welcoming, and this can be fantastic for someone who is traveling alone for several weeks.

Now that we've touched on the pros of staying in hotels, let's talk about potential cons. The downside can be that they tend to be a more expensive option, which is obviously the case if you are thinking about five-star luxury. For example, if you look at options in South Korea, you can find a decent hotel for a few dollars a night, or you can go right to the other end of the scale, choose someplace fancy and end up paying over $250 per night. It may be reckless, but no one can stop you – it's your money! Just remember that if you travel within a lower budget for accommodations, you will be able to travel for longer, and see and do more while you're there.

Another downside with hotels abroad can be this: if you have left your own home to travel the world and only stick to hotels, you may find yourself stuck inside the 'tourist bubble' – only seeing the world from a slightly distant and sanitized point of view, rather than really getting in amongst the locals.

So, if you are looking for a more richly textured experience and would like to explore outside of your comfort zone, look at alternative places to stay, or mix it up a little.

Hostels

Hostels can be found throughout the world, offering cheap accommodations for travelers who are typically young and on a budget – making them perfect for the YBP in many instances. Hostels offer basic boarding, mainly in dormitory-style rooms, so they may not be for you if you relish your privacy, though some do offer private rooms, too. Hostels tend to be clean and safe, and they can be a great place to meet like-minded travelers. Staying in hostels can ultimately save you a fortune on hotel bills. Zostel Jaipur in India starts at US$6.03 per night for a dorm bed, just as an example.

Even if you don't think of yourself as a hostel type of person, it could be well worth giving them a try. In some remote areas, you may have no other options anyway. Whatever your reason for staying in one, you may find your eyes opened to a whole new travel choice for the future. There may be no room service or other fancy amenities, but after you've trekked through the rainforest or up a mountain, all you may need is a dry bed and clean water.

Give them a try. I personally live by hostels- they are almost always the best fit for me while budget traveling.

Home Stays

These are designed, as their name to suggests, to offer home-style comfort at your destination. Most home stays would offer, for example, air-conditioned rooms, laundry and ironing services, 24-hour internet, satellite TV, and more, often for about US$20 per night. Some may offer a breakfast service, others may not. You will have a host who will oversee your stay and make sure you have everything you need, acting as a useful point of contact.

Home stays can be great to use as a reliable, comfortable base from which you can explore the surrounding area. They can also be perfect for longer-term stays or trip where you have to be in contact with the outside world – for example, they are often popular with traveling journalists.

You will be in touch with the local owner and they may be able to give you invaluable tips to the local attractions and sights. As a comfortable and usually low-cost option that still gives you access to the local culture on your doorstep, home stays can be fantastic. Note that they may have different variations and names throughout the world. In Europe you may choose between a guesthouse or B&B (Bed and Breakfast) or a serviced apartment, in Cuba it is called a *casa particuliere.*

Home stays can give your trip a great level of warmth and comfort – you may also make a friend in the owner, so keep an open mind and choose one to suit your tastes.

TIP – Whatever style of accommodations you go for, make sure you shop around for bargains. Sites like <u>www.hostels. com</u> offer some great deals for US travelers, or you may be able to get a low rate by contacting the hotel, hostel, or home stay directly. I personally read all the comments left by previous guests, and that helps me narrow down my selection.

From Luxury to Lucked Out (and everything in between)

As a consumer you have choices, choices, and more choices. You now know the types of accommodation that are available in most parts of the world, but it's time to ask yourself the question: should you blow half of your budget on an upscale hotel, or go as cheap as you dare?

There are obvious advantages to luxury – first-class service, spacious and well-appointed rooms, swimming pools, air-conditioning, room service, the best food and drink, a concierge service… but frankly, if you could afford all that, all of the time, you wouldn't need a travel book for the Young Broke Professional!

The reality is that while most of us can feel very at home in luxurious surroundings, our budgets won't always allow for us to enjoy the indulgence of five-star accommodations.

On the other hand, if you go right to the other end of the scale, you don't want to be living in dangerous, unsanitary conditions. A clean, safe bed and clean water is a must. Toilet facilities, a mosquito net, somewhere to wash and keep your things where you feel comfortable that they won't get stolen can seem like all the 'five-star' accommodation you need when you are touring some of the more remote parts of Africa, for example.

In the end, it's all a balance. I would always rather opt for a longer trip and not overspend on where I was staying. What you can do, if you like a taste of luxury on your travels, is spend the majority of your time abroad staying in budget accommodations, like a hostel. Then on the last night or two, when you are gearing up to go home, spend a couple of nights in a luxurious (or at least more comfortable) hotel in the airport town; if you can afford it, why not? It will be a real treat and acclimatize you to returning home.

Maximize Your 'Welcome Guest' Factor

There is nothing like staying with a friend to enjoy a relaxed and truly authentic stay. Genuine home comfort, staying with someone we know and trust, and receiving all the inside information on the area…this is the ideal situation. Unfortunately, most of us don't have a friend in every country we could visit (although that would not be a bad goal to set for yourself). Still, there is nothing stopping you for asking around – you will be surprised how easy it is to find a known contact in the country you want to visit.

For the determined YBP who wants to spend serious amounts of time traveling, as well as the ones who just want to hop across the pond for a few days, there is nothing better than a personal recommendation. Speak to family, friends, and colleagues to see if they know anyone who happens to be living in Costa Rica, Martinique, Nairobi, Dubai, or New Zealand…wherever. They might just have a friend of a friend who is willing to put you up for free. This is much more common practice than you might realize and can cut more than half the cost of your trip – so don't be shy, ask!

Of course, if your friends are not that globally connected, there are other things that you can do to source free accommodation. Write to charitable organizations offering your services, in exchange for a room or bed; write to academic institutions offering English support, in exchange for free or low cost student accommodation.... get creative! Use your imagination and remember what we YBPs always say – if you don't ask, you won't receive!

Big Bad World?

Too many Americans worry about the world around them. It's understandable; we live on such huge continent. Everywhere else seems distinctly foreign, and with good reason – it is. Our TV screens bring tales of international crime and disorder into our living rooms on a daily basis. No wonder we worry. But should that be enough to stop us from buying a ticket to paradise?

Realistic v Alarmist Safety Considerations

There are certain thing that you should think about before and during your travels, and certain aspects to forget about altogether. Knowing which is which can make the difference between a truly great trip and one that is just 'ok'.

> **DO – Look after your money and passport**. You are more likely to lose cash than to have it stolen, but even in the safest environments there may be unscrupulous or desperate people on the lookout for easy pickings like unguarded wallets. Of course, if you live in a big US city, you will be well aware of the need to always keep an eye on your things. Even so, it can be easy to get too relaxed in

beautiful locations abroad. Just try to keep a sensible mixture of ready cash and credit cards – plus always leave one card stashed in your room – and you will be fine even if you lose your wallet.

DON'T – Be overly-cautious about strangers. Nearly everyone you meet while traveling abroad will be a stranger, so you may need to adjust your ideas about what is safe and what is not. In most countries, if you go with your gut and trust recommended people, you are likely to have a great time. Let's say a man comes up to you and says that for the equivalent of a dollar in local currency, he will lead you to the most beautiful rainforest gorge, where a 100 foot waterfall cascades down. Would you go? It you're a woman traveling solo and he's a man, probably not. If he's over 60 and you're in a group of three, maybe you will. It's all about judging each situation on its merits.

DO – Try the unknown. You may never have heard of *accra morue*, or seen a real-life snake charmer in the middle of a bustling *souk*. You might not have realized that deep down, you had an urge to try parasailing, or wear a sari, or ride a camel. However, when these opportunities come your way, don't hold back. Of course, you will want to ensure a basic level of safety, but most everything in life is a risk, so be adventurous!

DON'T – Be a tourist. There are different ways to see a country. One is as a local, another is a tourist. What you want to be is a traveler.

Tourists stay firmly ON the beaten path. They buy package holidays, tip well for unnecessary services and never stray far from the pool. They may very much enjoy a country, but they never really get under its skin.

Travelers are different. They view themselves as global citizens and try to find things to love and identify with everywhere they visit. They want to love what the locals love, not some specially laid out tourist attraction. They want to swim the rivers, hug the elephants, taste the national delicacies, and dance like no one's watching. Don't hold back – be a genuine traveler.

DO- Always let someone know where you are going. This is important. Don't even think about going on that hour-long mountain stroll or wandering off into a jungle without letting someone know exactly what you're doing. It is ok; I know you're a grown-up. But even the most competent adults can get lost or otherwise get into difficulties. It is simply stupid to go off without at least letting the hotel owner know where you are. Text a friend if you must, but when traveling solo,

SOMEONE should know where you are at all times. We've all seen those bulletins on the 10 o'clock news where some unfortunate traveler has disappeared. Stay in contact, even when you want time alone…and stay safe.

Why More Americans Have A Passport Than Ever Before:

We used to be famous for it as a country: never traveling. Our European cousins once viewed the average American as someone who never strayed away from their (admittedly huge) natural home.

They were right, up to a point, but that was a long time ago. In 1989, only 7 million Americans, a shocking 3 percent, even owned a passport! Isn't that incredible?

Now though, it is a different picture. More Americans than ever own a passport, an admirable 110 million people, or over 33 percent of the population, according to Forbes.

This has to be a welcome progression. After all, just like everyone else on the planet, we only get one life and we don't necessarily want to spend every minute of it safely ensconced in the Land of the Free. There's a big, wide world out there, and as a YBP with a case of wanderlust, you, like me, will be delighted that more people are choosing to explore it.

On the other hand, in recent years, Americans have had some concerns about how they are perceived by the locals in certain countries. We worry about what we hear on the news and think that we might just be seen as walking ATMs by some locals. The short answer is to be friendly, never arrogant, and you might be surprised at how friendly even the most under-privileged and culturally different people can be toward Western strangers.

If you have never had a passport, you are on the threshold of an incredible new phase of life. Just imagine: it's Thursday night and you are sick of being home in Seattle. You are longing for the romance and tradition of Paris and have a few hundred dollars to spare. Within hours you could book a flight and be there, reciting Baudelaire's poetry as you stroll down some lovely boulevard, croissant in hand!

OK, so you might not want to hop off to Paris, but the point is, with a passport, you absolutely *can*. How about London, Delhi, Johannesburg, Sydney, or Bora Bora? All you need is a passport, and in some cases, a visa.

One last thing on this subject, which is close to the hearts of all cosmopolitan Americans, spread the word. As the number one rich, industrialized nation, we should go out there and try to understand this world of which we are viewed as being the leader. It is a responsibility that comes with global privilege…but is also a fantastic amount of good fun!

Once we get truly inside other cultures, we can understand them, and use this understanding to enrich our lives. So, if you have a friend or family member without a passport, have a word with them and encourage them to embrace the joy of travel!

Don't Worry Be Happy - Mugging and Other Myths

We sometimes fear that the world is a big, bad place. It can be, but I'm a huge believer in the fact that most people are good, and want to enjoy the company of other good people.

I know quite a few people who can't understand why I am not scared when I travel. They ask me why I don't worry and see me as 'brave' when I travel alone.

If you ask me, this is entirely the wrong focus.

Yes, of course we need to stay safe, whether in Brooklyn or Belize. But traveling doesn't automatically make life more dangerous.

Just like there are across the USA, there are crime hotspots abroad as well:

Don't, for example, go wandering around Cape Town, South Africa alone at night, whether you are male or female (especially female).

Don't try to make friends with drug dealers in Caracas – this is not an episode of *Homeland*.

If you have heard about it on the news – Iraq, Yemen, Somalia, Syria – then give it a wide berth. War zones… certain places in the Middle East…probably not the best places for Americans at the moment.

YBPs are generally smart, and I'd be surprised if any of the readers of this book were planning to take unnecessary risks, even if some may work for charitable organizations or wish to help disadvantaged people.

The key to this is research, research, research. Look online to find the US government's latest advice about traveling to your chosen destination. It is usually accurate and up-to-the-minute. Listen to it and plan accordingly.

There you have it, that's as much doom and gloom as there needs to be.

The world and its people are miraculous. Don't be afraid of it.

This brings me to another subject – traveling alone. Some people, especially women, are shocked when I reveal the places I have ventured to on my own. It always amuses them. Any YBP can mitigate the risks and do their best to keep themselves safe, whether they are traveling as a lone woman, or a member of a group.

There are certain considerations to bear in mind when you do not have a travel companion. There are also huge rewards to be enjoyed from traveling solo.

Here are my top five reasons why you should travel alone at least once in your life:

1. **All of the amazing people you will meet**
   While traveling with friends or a significant other can be fun, traveling alone proves to be one of the most

rewarding things you'll ever do, largely because of all of the people you will meet. I can't tell you how many times I have traveled alone and met the most wonderful people in my host country, and they helped make my trip incredible! When you travel alone, it forces you step outside of your comfort zone and meet new people.

2. **Solo traveling helps you grow up**
   In my opinion, maturity doesn't come with age, it comes with experience. There have been many times I have been put in situations where I had to make mature, sound decisions while traveling solo. You don't get to hide behind someone else's decision. I have had to budget money, make decisions that would ensure my safety, and plan and organize my days while on the road. These tasks played a huge role in my growth as an individual.

3. **You can do exactly what you want, when you want!**
   All our lives, we are taught that it is not okay to be selfish; well, solo traveling is the exception to that rule! When I am traveling solo, I wake up when I want to, eat when I want to, sightsee when I want to, etc. Solo traveling allows me to experience traveling my way!

4. **It helps you get over your fears**
   Once, while traveling in Costa Rica, I realized I had so many small fears that I wasn't willing to admit to back home. I was afraid of being alone and I was afraid of taking risks. I realized I was literally carrying my fears around the world with me and that it had to stop. When you are traveling alone, you get to think, and

think some more! The thinking never stops! This allows you the time you need to deal with whatever issues you may be having in your personal life.

5. Learn to be alone and be happy

I am a very outgoing, people-loving individual. I'd so much rather be with a group of friends than be alone. Traveling solo has shown me an alternative to filling my time with tons of people, though. I have truly learned the art of being alone and happy, whether I am sitting at a café reading a book, or people watching. It took some time for me to understand that I had to be happy alone before I could truly be happy around others.

...Other Travel Myths to Ignore

This section should finally put to bed any fears you might have about the 'Big, Bad World'.

Travelers get ripped off – This is a very common myth, particularly among Americans and Europeans. The truth is, yes, if you go to the wrong places, you may be charged ridiculous prices for average food, be forced to pay twice the usual taxi fare, and miss out on some of the advantages that the locals take for granted.

But this is far more likely to happen if you act like a *tourist,* not a *traveler.* Don't walk around in designer T-shirts or flashing expensive jewelry – it is asking for trouble. Don't over-tip to impress the staff, unless you plan to spend the whole time in a 5-star hotel – it gives the wrong impression.

Be smart, shop around, do what the locals do. There may be a restaurant that is packed with other American tourists...but have you tried the restaurant that has the locals lining up around the block? Guess which one is likely to have the better local food?

If you keep your wits about you and listen to your new local friends, you can easily avoid the rip-offs. Naturally, the longer you stay in one place, the easier this is to do, so spend proper time at your destination (like you needed an excuse)!

The roads/ trains/ planes are dangerous overseas - Transport anywhere can be precarious, but you knew that. If you are visiting Europe, you don't need to worry too much. The standards are incredibly high in most Western European countries, such as England, France, and Germany (Eastern European infrastructure is developing and less well-funded). Beyond Europe, you may find the some of the transport 'interesting'. Once you have traveled on an Indian train where people sit on the roof and hang off of the sides, you will never complain about a packed commuter train again!

On the whole, as a Westerner (and usually comparably rich, even as a YBP) you can make all the smart choices about transport. You will never have to take a flight with the airline that has the worst safety record on that continent. You will never have to get into a taxi where the limping car has clearly never been serviced, and where the driver smells strongly of whisky. You are traveling for pleasure, and can always say no.

But happily, such experiences are few and far between. We may all come from different countries, but on the whole, we all still want to live well and safely. Undoubtedly, life can feel more cheap in some countries than others, but if you plan ahead and choose to take the smart options, you can enjoy hassle-free travel all around the world, as surely and safely as if you were taking a cable car in San Francisco.

Foreigners hate Americans – This is nonsense. If you listen to the news every night, you could be thinking this, but apart from some places in the Middle East (which are dangerous for any Westerner, of any color or religion), you are more likely to be embraced with joy. People may well be very curious though – my blonde friend was amazed by the amount of interest she attracted in Marrakech, simply walking through the marketplace to get to her luxury *riad* (a *riad* is a traditional Moroccan house or palace, with an interior garden or courtyard).

Just relax and smile – it's an international language.

The food will be terrible – Call me lucky, but I have found the opposite to be true! All you have to do is pick good, clean restaurants and cafes, etc. Of course, everyone loves Momma's home cooking, but beyond the shores of the USA, there are a whole lot of delicious cuisines to tuck into.

I have made no secret of the fact that I adore Indian food. What I really loved discovering, though, is that Indian food is one thing in the U.S., and entirely something else – largely vegetarian - in its home country. There are also stand-out dishes that define a country, like the *mofongo* I tried in Puerto Rico, or the many Jamaican treats I tried in Negril.

Food when you travel is *amazing*! Don't be put off by the pessimists – seize the day and try foods you have never tasted before. Bon appétit!

Lone Ranger

We've taken a brief look at the idea of traveling alone, but it deserves its own chapter as so many YBPs give the matter considerable thought. The main question that comes up in relation to solo travel is the timeless one:

Is it Safe to Travel Alone?

My short answer is, "yes." Or to be more precise, "yes, but…"

Traveling alone can be one of the greatest adventures you will ever experience. The article in the previous chapter has outlined a few great reasons why – the new people, the freedom, and so on. Now we will look a little more closely at *how* to travel alone…and safety has to be a primary consideration.

To get started, let's look at the facts – the vast majority of travelers experience no crimes or problems whatsoever. You are likely to be one of them, and you can increase your chances of a trouble-free trip by following these top 10 safety tips:

1. Be alert in and around tourist attractions. Pickpockets and other petty criminals often hide

in crowds, waiting for unsuspecting victims. Stay aware.

2. Always keep an eye on your belongings – even if you pop into the sea for a dip, to make sure your things are safe.
3. Avoid the crime hotspots and never visit downtown areas of large cities alone, especially after dark.
4. Don't walk around wearing expensive jewelry, as you may attract the wrong sort of people.
5. Similarly, don't carry a lot of cash or make it obvious that you have money on you – this could be asking for trouble.
6. Don't show muggers where your valuables are; keep your things hidden as much as possible.
7. Don't get visibly drunk on your own – this will make you more vulnerable, as criminals often target drunken tourists.
8. Keep your handbag/man bag physically attached to you at all times, even putting a foot through the strap when it is resting on the floor to keep it safe.
9. Don't wander aimlessly – look as though you know where you're going, and if you don't, go discreetly into a café to check a map.
10. Don't hitchhike – it's been a no-no for years, but a surprising number of travelers think it is an acceptable mode of transport. If you are alone it is simply too dangerous – you'd be better off walking.

Planning Solo Travels

Like most aspects of traveling, when you travel alone, you will find it safer, and more enjoyable if you plan ahead.

Make sure that you:

ALWAYS – Let someone know where you are and where you're going, whether it's for a whole three-week trip to Thailand or a short walk through the park at home.

MAKE SMART PLANS - Try to ensure that the plans you make will not leave you in a risky place or short of cash. While travel is an adventure, when you are alone you need to make sure all bases are covered.

DO MAKE FRIENDS – Speak to friends and family and you might be surprised to find that they know someone else who is traveling to the same region as you at the same time. By the same token, research trustworthy internet contacts. It can really help to pair up with people or join a group at certain points in your trip.

IN CASE OF EMERGENCY - Hopefully you won't encounter any emergency situations, but if you should, you need to be prepared. Firstly, keep an emergency stash of money someone that no one but you will look. A $100 bill hidden away could prove to be priceless.

Secondly, in case of an accident, you need to make sure it is easy for people to contact your loved ones. Keep an ICE (In Case of Emergency) phone number on your mobile phone.

Thirdly, learn in advance where to go for urgent help if you should need it. You should know each country's equivalent of 911 wherever you go and, closer to hand, make sure you know how to get hold of the hotel or hostel staff if you need them.

Never Be Lonely

A more likely danger than being mugged is that of feeling lonely when traveling solo, particularly if it is for a long period of time. Human beings are naturally sociable animals, and that doesn't change when you are on the other side of the world – quite the opposite.

Follow these tips, and you will be able to enjoy the best of being alone and have more fun, too:

- Think carefully about your accommodations - hostels are great for mixing with other YBPs, and you will probably find them to be more sociable than ritzy hotels or many resorts.
- Do think about traveling by train - you could make some amazing friends (or even start a new romance) in the dining car!
- Enjoy organized tours with guides, as many solo travelers flock to these to soak up some culture.
- Chat with strangers – there is nothing like a great conversation to stop loneliness in its tracks and reconnect you with the rest of the species.

- Find an activity that will attract like-minded YBPs. You might want to go to a local dance class like salsa or tango, or take some language classes. Learn a new skill and make new friends at the same time.
- Go to canteen-style restaurants where you all sit at communal tables. These can be great environments for striking up friendly conversations and meeting other hungry fellow travelers.
- Spend time at internet cafes or wherever you can get free Wi-Fi. These places attract YBPs like moths to a flame. Plus, you will be able to update your social media accounts, stay in touch with loved ones, and feel far less lonely.
- Become a regular – keep visiting the same bar, same restaurants, etc. When you start being recognized as a regular, you will get a warmer welcome, as well as feeling more at home.
- Dance, go to parties, and enjoy the nightlife. You will have a ton of fun and might enjoy some great new encounters along the way.

Remember, when it comes to traveling solo, safety comes first…then fun will soon follow!

Play It Smart

As a student, both in college and graduate school, I made sure to take advantage of any opportunity that presented itself for me to travel abroad, and you should too! If you are still in school, then this information is just for you!

1. University Partnerships: Sometimes your school may have a partnership with other schools in other countries where you could have the opportunity to go take classes for a week or two, or maybe even an entire semester
2. Let your professors know your interest in traveling: Make sure you tell your professors, advisors, and teacher's aides about your desire to go abroad. I made my professors very aware that I wanted to travel, which led to me being able to complete a semester of school online and apply for a summer fellowship, where I was paid *and* awarded free housing to participate in a critical language program.
3. STUDY ABROAD!

Studying Abroad – A Different Way to Travel

YBPs can travel for many different reasons and in a variety of ways. If you don't think you have a valid 'reason' for spending a period of time in another country, maybe due to the fact that you are in the middle of your studies, you might seriously want to consider enjoying some time studying abroad.

Secure Travel Opportunities Through School Programs

If you are still a student, you have a great advantage at your fingertips. Check with your university to see if (and where) they run summer, winter, or yearlong study abroad programs. You can also look into other organizations which can also help you study abroad:

AIFS: http://www.aifsabroad.com/
CEA: http://www.ceastudyabroad.com/default.html
CIEE: http://www.ciee.org/
CISabroad: http://www.cisabroad.com/study-abroad
Global Links: http://www.globalinksabroad.org/

Travel and education have huge amounts in common because they both broaden your horizons and broaden the mind. You may have put the idea off because you thought it would be too difficult to organize, but if you take a look at some useful websites, you will see it is pretty straightforward.

Follow their guidelines and enroll directly to gain access to their programs.

Pros and Cons of Studying Abroad

College life is already pretty exciting. For many of us, it is the first time we are living away from home and packed with fun, freedom, and opportunities. For more adventurous students, you may find that there are even great unexpected opportunities – like the chance to travel the world and enjoy a completely unique experience.

Unsurprisingly, I am all for YBPs traveling as soon as they are able, including during their college years. However, there are some considerations to bear in mind before jetting off abroad.

Here's a mixture of pros and cons to bear in mind when considering study abroad (here's a hint though – I believe that the PROS totally outweigh the CONS, naturally!):

PRO – You Can Experience a Foreign Culture

There is nothing like having your own experience of travel to feel like you are really living. It is all very well to admire the plains of South Africa in a film, or to climb Amazonian waterfalls in your imagination when you read a book, but there really is nothing like being there in person. Travel can surprise all your senses, often all at once, and it can be a real thrill to immerse yourself in the customs and culture of other people.

PRO – Learn a New Language

If you have some basic Spanish, why not enhance it with a few months in Barcelona? Or hone your French skills in Paris, Mauritius, or Martinique? There are endless opportunities for improving a language or learning a new one from scratch. Just remember – there is no better way to learn a language than by chatting with locals every day. You will pick up authentic words, gain fluency, and improve your confidence – so dive in!

CON – You May Feel Homesick

This is something that many travelers experience if they stay abroad for a long period of time. You may find yourself surrounded by some of the best scenery on a brand new continent, but unable to think of anything apart from your family back home. The trick is not to panic or despair – just get in touch and let them know you're missing them. These days, with Wi-Fi and internet it is easier than ever to stay in touch. However, it is a good idea not to stay constantly in contact with the folks back home – give yourself a chance to become really immersed in the country that you have traveled so far to see, and you will ultimately feel less homesick.

PRO – Trying New Activities

There is nothing like travel to make someone feel more adventurous. Eating a plate of snails may sound like a terrible idea on a Wednesday night in Wisconsin, but try them on a beautiful afternoon in Burgundy, and your opinion could be transformed! The same goes for bungee-jumping, wind-surfing, parasailing or whatever you fancy. It does not necessarily have to be an adventure sport – perhaps you have always wanted to try oil painting - your six months in Tuscany will be the perfect opportunity.

CON – May Not Receive Enough Financial Aid to Cover Program

One of the most common issues shared by those who want to study abroad is that they do not have enough financial aid to cover the cost. For example: If you receive $10,000 in federal financial aid, but you wish to study abroad on a $15,000 program, how could you come up with the remainder of the balance?

Answer:

1. Choose a study abroad program with a lower cost. There are plenty of summer or semester programs for less than, or right around $10,000, in some beautiful countries. Choose one of those instead.
2. To avoid sticker shock, make sure you focus on the TRUE costs of studying abroad. For example: If you receive $10,000 in financial aid and you choose a $15,000 program, the TRUE cost to you would be $5,000. If you have planned in advance, it is very feasible to save up $5,000 the year before you are set to study abroad (i.e. working a part-time or full-time job, fundraising, applying for study abroad scholarships/grants, etc.).

Study Abroad Scholarship Websites:

http://www.studyabroad.com/scholarships.aspx
http://www.nafsa.org/Explore_International_Education/
For_Students/U_S_Study_Abroad_Scholarships_and_
Grants_List/
http://www.gooverseas.com/
blog/65-study-abroad-grants-and-scholarships

PRO – Discover Your Roots

You may have an interesting cultural background, such as a parent from another country. Study abroad in your ancestral home and get to know your roots! Your time abroad could turn out to be one of the most amazing times in your personal life, and a very significant way to strengthen family bonds, as well as a great adventure.

PRO - You Will Become More Independent

One of the best – and at first one of the scariest – thing about studying aboard is that your normal life is changed and you can no longer rely on your usual support network. This is a good thing! You will learn to be more resourceful, to challenge yourself, to use your judgment, and to make smart choices. In a new country, even buying groceries can be a challenge at first, but as you succeed in different small tasks, you will become more and more confident. Relish your new independence; it is precious and as close as you can get to real freedom.

PRO – Become a Real Catch for Employers

If you are the owner of a successful, international company, and you want to hire a bright, independent graduate, who is more likely to pique your interest: a smart student who has done nothing but study in the town in which they were born, or another smart student who has studied just as hard, but also traveled abroad, been independent for months, risen to all kinds of challenges, and possibly even learned a new language? No brainer!

Check out my blog extract at the end of the chapter to find out just how employable you can become.

CON - Travel Can Be Expensive

That can be true, but part of the joy of being a YBP is that you have great books like *Wanderlust* to help you travel for less. Eating out, transportation, and generally living abroad can certainly add up, but you can take major steps to maximize your income, like applying for grants and scholarships. In the end, you have to do everything you can to lower the costs, but you should also simply view travel as an investment in your own future.

PRO – Make New Friends

Connecting with great people surely has to be the best thing on earth, right? When you travel, you will be given unique opportunities to make friends with all kinds of people, some of whom may be more interesting and surprising that you would have ever expected! The exciting thing is that until you get out there and start traveling, you will never know who you will meet – it could be a new friend for life…

Five Most Cost-Effective Countries in Which to Study

Studying abroad is such an exciting option…but as a YBP, you need to make sure that you are getting the best possible value for money. This doesn't just mean tuition fees, but also the cost of living and other associated expenses. One company, StudyCostCompare, has provided the latest data on the best countries to study in, taking into account the average costs of tuition fees, shopping and transport:

1. *Italy*

   The oldest university in the world – the University of Bologna, founded in 1088 - is in this superb country. With a great pedigree and lots of other top universities, plus as it offers the lowest cost of living among the better study abroad destinations, Italy is a first-class choice. Not to mention the amazing food, architecture, art, countryside, and language...

2. *Spain*

   More than 70 universities offer a wide range of choice at very affordable rates. Perfect your Spanish as you enjoy a course that feels just made for you. The general cost of living in Spain is also very affordable and the culture is lively, friendly, vibrant, and warm.

3. *Germany*

   Germany is a top European study destination, with a higher cost of living than some countries, but low tuition fees and very high standards. This makes studying abroad here an exceptionally good value for money. There are over 350 universities and 800 courses, plus the country is cosmopolitan, comfortable, and easy to travel around.

4. *Denmark*

An innovative, exciting, and forward-thinking country, Denmark has high standards of education. The landscapes are beautiful, the people are interesting, and fees and cost of living are low, making Denmark a great place to study with a difference.

5. *New Zealand*

One of the most striking things about New Zealand is its incredible natural beauty. If you love an outdoors lifestyle and want a first-rate education, this could be the country for you. The University of Auckland and the University of Otago are both featured in the QS Top 200 World Universities. It is a nation of independent thinkers, and the fees are relatively low, so if you think you could thrive in the visually stunning land where Lord of the Rings was filmed, don't hold back...

However, at the end of the day you have to ask yourself - why? Why study abroad at all?

Well, if my PROs didn't hook you in and you were worried about the potential cons in the previous list, perhaps it is time you look at a little piece I wrote in reference to the valuable skills I learned while traveling during my gap year after finishing school.

Anyone concerned about becoming more employable through travel should listen up...

The 5 Most Employable Skills I Learned From Traveling During My Gap Year

After graduating with my master's degree, I decided that I wanted to take some time off from work and life to complete a gap year- a year full of traveling, writing a book, and discovering my life's passions. I feared many people would think a gap year at that point of my life was crazy considering I was a 26-year-old recent graduate who had the type of job my parents described as a 'good government job,' but I wasn't happy or fulfilled. I had been in school since age six and I had done everything I was supposed to in life by that point- so I decided I would finally embark on something that I truly wanted to do. I took every penny I had to my name and financed a year doing things that only brought fulfillment, meaning, and pleasure to my life. If I told you I wasn't scared or nervous, I would have been telling a big lie, and the fact that I had never met anyone else who looked like me do something like this made me even more fearful - but I knew I had to do this. I budgeted, planned, made phone calls, consulted with friends and mentors, started a blog, and put a plan in action. During my gap year I traveled to South Africa, Hawaii, Mexico, New Orleans, the Bahamas, Key West, California, and Georgia, and ended 2013 by planning a 40-day solo travel trip throughout Thailand, Bali, Australia and Fiji. Words can't express how much I learned last year. No I didn't go to a formal "9 to 5" every day, nor did I have a boss or coworkers, but the lessons I learned from traveling far exceeded anything I could have learned working in a corporate setting for 12 months.

1. Budgeting

This is the question I get asked the most: 'How could you afford to not work for a year?' Well, the short answer to that question is extreme saving and budgeting. I worked full-time while in graduate school and lived below my means for quite some time, which helped me save a significant amount of money. I also cut down on cable, cell phone bills, car insurance, etc. I took advantage of every discount and promotion I could. Smart budgeting was very important to the success of my gap year, so I gave myself a monthly allowance, I got rid of all major bills (read more about this in my book), and I only traveled if I found a great deal. Now, I can most certainly use my budgeting skills in any career role I wish.

2. Time Management Skills

A job skill I see on almost every vacancy posting is great multi-tasking and time management skills. What better way to prove that you have this acquired skill than by showing you took the time to research, make an outline, plan and execute time to travel, volunteer, or whatever else you decided to do? Not only that, but when traveling you have to be punctual to ensure you don't miss buses, planes, and trains. You must also be very organized with your passport, hotel reservations, transfer tickets, and more! A gap year of traveling definitely builds universal time management skills.

3) Writing Skills

One of the first things I did when I knew I was about to embark on my gap year was start a blog. I wanted a way to connect with people before, during, and after my travels. The year before I began my gap year, I blogged while living in India for two months (deidreinindia.wordpress.com) and it was a success, so I knew I had to start a new one. In May of 2013, www.passportsandpizzazz.com was born.

Writing is a universal skill. No matter what level, role, or position you are in, at some point you will be required to use some form of written communication. I can now boast to employers that I have over a year of writing samples on my blog.

4) Diversity & People Skills

This is a very diverse world we live in, and it is important to know how to work with any and every one. Traveling has given me the skills to be able to do just that. Whether I was lost in Fiji, sick in Thailand, or handling financial matters at the bank in South Korea, dealing with language barriers is something with which I am extremely comfortable! Imagine how comfortable I am with those that speak my language! I believe that real life experience is very important, and my diverse people skills would be an enhancement to any organization.

5) Adaptability

Nothing says adaptability more than traveling to a foreign place alone! During my 40-day solo trip, I had to adapt to places quickly, safely, and efficiently. Most employers want to know that you will be able to come onboard, learn the material, be independent, and adapt to the company's environment - I can't think of a better way to prove adaptability than traveling solo.

As with so many things in life, travel experiences have taught me to push myself beyond what I would ever have thought possible if I had just stayed at home in the States.

It can be just the same for you, as a YBP who wants to see the world. Get out there to travel, study, explore, and experience; by the time you get back, you will be twice the person you were when you left!

Cruising 101

The Cruising Lowdown

Ever wondered whether going on a cruise would be a wonderful experience, or one to be avoided at all costs? Take a look at this must-read lowdown on cruising…

One Vacation, Many Destinations

Why cruise? Well, for most people the reason for cruising consists of more than an overwhelming love of big ships. It's more about the chance to do something completely different, and the biggest perk of all is the fact that cruising can mean one vacation with many destinations – which means fantastic fun!

If you are not familiar with cruises, the basic concept is this – you choose an area of the world and an available length of time. Then you hop on board and visit each of the countries in which you dock, as you wish, until you return home. One sample cruise of the Caribbean may include these ports of call, for example:

New York - Cape Liberty, Bayonne, New Jersey - Labadee, Haiti - San Juan, Puerto Rico - Philipsburg, St. Maarten - St.

Johns, Antigua - Basseterre, St. Kitts, Cape Liberty, Bayonne, New Jersey – New York

Sounds great!

So, if geographic coverage is important to you, then a cruise could easily be the best way to maximize your travel fun.

However, as mentioned, you have to bear in mind that cruises can be expensive, unless you look in the right place. There are some generalist companies and cruise lines which have been highlighted as value for money, such as Carnival Cruises. Carnival has all-inclusive offers and low costs all-around value, with mainly British and American passengers.

However, if you are serious about saving money, you need discount cruise services, such as:

http://www.americandiscountcruises.com/
http://cruises.priceline.com/promotion/cruise-deals.do
http://www.top-cruise-deals.com/

These sites slash the prices of regular cruises, and can save you hundreds of dollars if you browse around.

Cruising for YBPs

There are some very expensive cruises, and there are also some that seem to be exclusively populated by older adults, but there are far more these days that are perfect for a YBP - great food, great destinations, and great value.

Not surprising that plenty of people under the age of 30 would consider a cruise these days.

Still not sure if a cruise is your thing? Here are a few quick pros and cons:

Cruise Pros

1. All-inclusive (with the exception of adult beverages)
2. Pre-planned activities for entertainment
3. Lots of people on board to befriend/ networking opportunities

Cruise Cons

1. You sometimes only have a few hours in each port to enjoy your destination
2. You may be affected by motion sickness
3. Some people have reported feeling "trapped" onboard after a few days

On the whole though, I'd say – go for it! If you are not in a hurry to get to one particular destination, why not take advantage of the onboard hospitality that cruise lines offer and enjoy a floating world of fun? You'll make friends and relax as you effortlessly travel the world. You may not opt for a cruise every time you go abroad, but it's worth trying at least once, for an eager YBP.

To make sure you get the most bang for your buck, follow my Top 10 Tips below to ensure better value cruising.

Top 10 Tips for a Super-Saver Cruise

If you choose wisely, there may be huge travel savings to be had by opting for a cruise. All your costs, from meals to entertainment, are bundled into one rate, which you've settled upfront. So no need for tricky budgeting and no hidden costs – just peace of mind as you cruise the world.

However, you do need to take some care if you want to enjoy the best possible value cruise:

1. Get picky with the price. Shop around for top value deals, not just on cruise lines' and travel agencies websites, but also social media pages and specialized deal websites to see if you can get special discounts, offers, and upgrades. Just check the small print and ask questions – know exactly what you are getting for your cash.
2. Find a travel agent who specializes in cruises. This can save you hours of solo research and is the probably the best way to make sure you get top value for money for exactly the type of cruise you would like. Make sure the agent is affiliated to the Cruise Lines International Association (CLIA). Also, you should not have to pay any fees on top for the agent as that is usually covered by the cruise line – so it's win-win!
3. Don't try to get last-minute deals - book early. Cruise lines reward early birds with hooks like reduced rates, onboard credits, and cabin upgrades. Book at least six months ahead if you can, or longer if it is for a peak season trip. Also, you can get great deals during "wave season", January to March and

also during National Cruise Vacation Week, which occurs in October.

4. Cruise during shoulder season, which falls between high and low season, and boasts mild temperatures, smaller crowds, and critically reduced rates. You can often get the same sailing at a fraction of the cost it would be during high season. Try to be smart when it comes to the time of year that you book a cruise. Cruising the Mediterranean in October will be far cheaper that in July, as with cruising the Caribbean in late fall, toward the end of the hurricane season. This does not necessarily mean a rough or stormy cruise, as the ship will steer a course away from brewing storms – but it could mean a brilliant value cruise for you.

5. Check out the best airfare rates – don't forget about the cost of getting to your homeport. It can be better to book a flight through the cruise line to ensure they will wait for you if the flight is delayed, for example, but these flights are rarely the cheapest. If you can, leave from the nearest homeport from which you can drive, and save by avoiding paying for airfare.

6. Pick the best cabin for your needs. This may not necessarily be the absolute cheapest – there are some rock-bottom priced interior rooms with no windows or natural light, but do NOT pick one of these unless you are sure claustrophobia will not ruin your trip. However, if you only intend to sleep in your room and are fairly robust, go cheap as you can and enjoy your time on deck, knowing you have made great savings.

7. Look into booking your own excursions. Cruise line-arranged trips can feel more secure, but often come at a premium. Research your own independent on-shore trips, and you could save a lot of money.

8. Don't go for the fanciest, newest ship. Cruise lines charge a major premium to sail aboard the best ships in their fleet, and they reduce rates on the older vessels. Save money and you are likely not to really notice any reduction in comfort, service, or amenities. Safety measures will be just as rigorous amongst reputable cruise lines, so don't be put off – grab those lower fares.

9. Build up brand loyalty. Airlines look after their frequent flyers and cruise lines reward repeat passengers, too. Keep cruising with the same line and enjoy more return-trip booking incentives, promotions, and discounts.

10. Don't forget to buy travel insurance to protect your investment. If anything goes wrong, your cruise costs and airfare will be covered and this can be essential when traveling outside the U.S. This may seem like a way to spend more money, not less, but trust me- in the long run you will be glad you had insurance, even if it is just for the peace of mind.

Earn It, Save It... Then Go!

Are you dying to get going on your next trip? Good for you – but how much money have you saved already? If the answer is "not much," there is no need to panic; you still have time to build up a nice, big pile of income to see you through your travels. I'm not just talking about a couple of weeks away here, I mean enough money to see you through a fantastic gap year, for example. Read on…

Tips for How to Fund Your Gap Time Away

Set Up a Bank Account

Throughout your gap year, you will need reliable access to money in the form of a secure bank account. Why not open one right now? Put as much money as you can into this account in the months leading up to your gap year, and do NOT touch it until you start your trip. Choose carefully - get a free account with minimal charges and full international access, and you'll be well set up for your travels.

Get a Part-Time Job

See this as a real money making opportunity. You may still be a student, or already work a full-time job, but if you have the time, try to cram in some extra work to boost your income before you travel. A gap year is great motivation to save money and it can add up very quickly. A retail or hospitality job could be good, especially something like waiting tables when you can make extra money from tips, and might even get a free dinner every shift, saving even more money! Think outside of the box and get busy earning money- when you are enjoying the sunshine of a distant beach with a cocktail in your hand, you will not regret it.

Request Cash Presents

Get organized and start planning this in advance. Ask your family members for birthday and Christmas presents in pure, simple cash so that you can put it toward your gap year fund. If any of them really don't like giving money, ask them to buy something else essential that you need for your trip, such as clothing or a guide book. But cash is king.

Get eBay-ing

You probably have a lot of 'stuff' sitting around your home that you could live without. Some of it may even be quite valuable. If that is the case, you need to start selling if off, today. Get rid of old knick-knacks and clutter and turn them into a pile of gap year cash by selling them on eBay. You know it makes sense.

Get Sponsored

A number of organizations sponsor young people who would like to go abroad. Do some research and find out which one might consider sponsoring you. You are likely to need to focus on either an educational or charitable reason for your trip, and apply accordingly. You will not necessarily need to be working for this cause the whole time you are away – look into the criteria for your sponsors and be sure to stick close to their requirements. Play it right and you could end up with a lot more funding for your travels.

Save-Don't Spend

Try to rein in your spending in the lead up to your gap year. Don't waste money on things that you don't really need. For every 10 dollars you are tempted to spend, imagine just what that could buy you in Egypt, Kenya, or Amsterdam. Think of it as delayed spending and you are far more likely to be successful.

While You're Away...

Don't forget – there are many opportunities to earn money while you are traveling.

1. **Teach English**
   Job opportunities are all around the world, and in some cases, you don't need to be certified, you just need to be a native speaker. Some of the most popular English teaching jobs are in South Korea, Japan, Thailand, and China.

2. **Work in a Hostel**
   Hostels are always looking for people that are willing to work as a receptionist, plumber, or housekeeper, in exchange for free room and board. Most people work

about 20 hours a week at a hostel and another 20 at a paid gig, not a bad way to save money at all.

3. **Do online freelance work**
   Websites such as elance.com make it easy to earn extra money while away. Whether you proofread college student essays or become a virtual assistant for a small business owner, there are many different options to making money while traveling.

4. **Working Holiday Visas**
   Countries such as Australia, New Zealand, Canada, France, Iceland, and Hong Kong offer these to foreigners, generally those who are between the ages of 18 – 30. If you're in that age range, the working holiday visa might just be your best option to make money and travel. It allows you stay in a country for up to one year, and in some cases, to apply for and work in any position you want.

5. **Travel Blogging**
   Although becoming a high paid travel blogger is very competitive and tough, it can be done. Most bloggers make money from having advertisements on their blog. Usually, you just need plenty of followers (this can range from 15,000 people and up) and an interesting, creative blog, and you can start to seek out business relationships with companies looking to advertise to other world travelers on your website.

6. **Work with your company abroad**
   Arrange to get a job within your existing company that will allow you to work abroad at an international

office. Meeting your company's local need is a creative and practical way of traveling and earning at the same time.

7. Pick fruit
If you don't mind getting your hands dirty and doing hard work, picking fruit just may be the job for you! If you are fit and like the outdoors, it could be the perfect way to keep in shape and earn extra cash.

8. Resort work or summer camp work
This is hard work rather than easy travel, but resorts tend to be in beautiful locations. Why not earn some money on a resort at the beginning of your travels and then spend your earnings as you travel freely afterwards?

9. Work on a cruise ship
This is the perfect way to combine your passion for traveling with a consistent paycheck. You can decide to be a bartender, a waiter, even a cruise ship performer! Whatever you decide, kick back and relax knowing that not only are you building your travel résumé, but you are meeting people from all over the world every day, and getting paid to do so.

10. Au pair
If you are young and love children, becoming an au pair can offer great travel-as-you-earn opportunities.

Some of my personal experience of making money abroad has been:

1. Teaching English in South Korea via the EPIK program (https://www.epik.go.kr/index.do)
2. Obtaining an Australian Work Visa (http://www.immi.gov.au/work/pages/work.aspx)
3. Applying for and participating in paid research grants abroad

(http://www.maccae.org/
visit-to-taj-mahal-india-july-2012/)

So, you see, using your imagination and getting creative can help you earn cash as you travel. With more cash in your pocket you can decide to keep traveling or pay off old debt.

The Buffer Zone

There is one very important financial aspect of traveling – saving something for emergencies, or creating a monetary 'buffer'. This can make your day, like when you realize you have overspent for accommodation, or make your night, when you have an once-in-a-lifetime invitation to a great event you cannot otherwise afford... it could even save your life.

In short, never underestimate the importance of the buffer, an emergency stash of cash to see you through no matter what.

Before you travel, especially if it is somewhere risky, ensure that you have access to at least $1000 (or more relevantly, the price of a last minute flight home) in case of absolute emergency. This does not have to be a formal arrangement. It is just good to know that in case of dire urgency you will have access to a savings account/ an overdraft.

Money is the lifeblood of travel. Don't let it dry up.

Exchanging Money

Although getting the best deals with exchanging money depends on many factors, including which currencies you want to convert and which country you are traveling to, generally speaking exchanging your money AFTER you travel will provide you with a more favorable exchange rate.

As a foreigner abroad, you want to do whatever you need to not to be ripped off and to get the best value for money. Most of the time, no one will be deliberately trying to give you a bad deal on your currency exchange, it is simply up to you to shop around as effectively as possible.

Exchange rates can vary hugely, even between two banks on the same street, so do you research – you may end up saving yourself a lot of money!

The more common the currency is, the cheaper it will be. So, for example, if you are traveling from the USA to Ireland and want to buy some Euro there, you will pay less for it in Ireland, as this is the currency that you will find everywhere in Europe. At the same time, your American Dollars will become rare and valuable, which means that you will get more money for them.

Here are my rules for exchanging money before or during my trips abroad

1) I use ATMs for my day-to-day funds.

Although some banks have high fees to use foreign ATMs, not to mention adding on high foreign-transaction fees (Bank of America, for example, charges $5 per withdrawal plus a 3 percent premium on top of each withdrawal at a non-partner ATM), the ATM is still almost always the cheapest option for changing your money. I usually take out a hefty amount, enough to last me at least half of my trip, as soon as I land in the respective airport of the country I am visiting.

2) I use my credit card

Using my credit card gives me the peace of mind that if something goes wrong, I have a backup plan that could give me my money back. Although my bank (Suntrust) charges a small fee for using my credit card internationally, it is worth it, because usually the exchange rates are less than what they would be when withdrawing money from the ATM.

3) Carry emergency money

I always carry a $100 bill in some hidden part of my suitcase in case my purse is stolen or missing. (I also always pre-pay hostel or hotel arrangements, so shelter will already be covered). This would allow me to pay for transportation, food, etc. until a replacement card comes to me, or until I can get money wired to me. You should never, ever travel without back up money!

4) Never take a cash advance on your credit card except in a dire emergency.

As Doug Stallings says on www.fodors.com, "If you take cash from a foreign ATM, you will pay a fee; you'll be charged a percentage on top of your withdrawal as a foreign-transaction charge; and you will start to pay very high interest (sometimes up to double the regular interest rate you are charged on your credit card) the moment the cash reaches your hands. It's a pretty bad deal. Avoid it at all costs unless you have no other choice."

5) I never ever sell my money at my local bank before traveling. I have had a few friends do this before taking a trip only to realize that the banks charge a very high fee for doing this, sometimes almost as much as 20 percent. Yes, it may be convenient, but it is literally throwing money down the drain. Don't do it!

There you have it - the lowdown on money before and during your travel abroad. Keep the financial lifeblood flowing and keep on traveling for as long as you wish!

Smooth Sailing

Trust me – while it's nice to sometimes "go with the flow" on vacation, you don't want to plan poorly and miss out on doing things that you won't get the opportunity to do again. My advice is to try to map out a few planned events in between your R&R. Planning ahead may even save you a few dollars. Here are a few more "before you go" tips.

1) Research Your Hotel:

See what amenities hotels in your travel destination offer. Do they offer free airport shuttles? Do they offer free breakfast in the morning? What about your hotel offering discounts on local restaurants or shopping malls? Knowing information like this can help you better choose what hotel to stay in, and may save money.

2) Have all of your documents prepared 48 hours in advance:

It is important for you to have your passports, flight information, and any other important documents organized at least two days before – NOT the day before your departure. If you plan to have your documents ready the night before and something does not go as planned (stuck in traffic, flat tire on car, etc.) you are more than likely going to rush and leave behind something important.

It is also essential to charge all electronics such as cameras, cell phones, iPods, etc. at least 24 hours before departure

3) Sign up for rewards points before you leave:

Nowadays, everyone offers some type of reward program: hotels, airlines, airport parking garages, and more. It is important to sign up to gain rewards point before you take off. Websites such as http://www.hotels.com offer a

"Stay 9 nights, get 1 free". I have used this program before and it has really helped me save money while traveling.

Airlines have awesome rewards programs! Earlier this year, I was able to get a free one way flight from Maryland to California by cashing in 25,000 airline miles I earned by traveling to and from India. If you travel frequently (or even if you take one really long flight), you can easily rack up tons of air credit.

Following these few suggestions can make your trip a whole lot easier and much more rewarding (literally)!

Packing Guide for YBPs

One big question of so many YBPs when they realize they are going to visit, let's say Greece- is: what will I wear? What should I bring? Do I really need five pairs of shoes? Those are all fair questions. After all, a travel wardrobe is dictated by climate, context, and your itinerary - not to mention your mood and personal style priorities, so this answer may vary from trip to trip.

However, packing well for real travel is a different matter altogether. You need to think light, practical, comfortable, and essential, with perhaps a splash of style all over, just for fun!

Here's a packing list for the average trip to Jamaica, for example:

Shorts
T-shirts
Comfortable walking shoes
Flip-flops
Water shoes
One pair of pants/skirt
Sweater for cool evenings
Insect repellant
Sunscreen

Swimwear
Underwear
Sarong
Sunglasses
One nice outfit for a dinner
Business cards if you have them (you never know who you will meet!)

This is pretty much it, although you can add and/or adapt according to the length of your stay and your exact location. The trick with packing is to focus on a core of essential items, or must-haves, and pack those first. When they are all in your suitcase, and only then, think about the nice-to-haves as secondary items. After all, whatever you do, you must not exceed the dreaded baggage allowance limits!

Don't Be Caught Over Weight – Baggage Limits

When you travel to most international destinations, you will be permitted to check at least one bag for free. If you go over, you will be charged.

There is nothing more infuriating than having to pay a surcharge because your baggage is over the limit. I avoid the costs by making sure that I am well aware of the airlines baggage allowances before I pack.

As an example, here is the Delta Airlines guidance on their baggage limits:

To avoid extra charges for oversize or overweight baggage, your checked bag must:
- weigh 50 pounds (23 kg) or less
- not exceed 62 inches (157 cm) when you total length + width + height

Each special item you check will count as one bag.

The best way to avoid ever having to pay for baggage is to get online and do your research and get organized. Over packing your luggage by even a few pounds could cause you to pay a fee of at least 50 dollars, depending on the airline!

Plan ahead and weigh your packed suitcase on your bathroom scale, or purchase a portable weight if you travel quite a bit. You can also learn how to efficiently pack everything in a carry-on suitcase, which is exactly what I do for every trip I take. This saves me money, time (once I reach the airport), and the stress of worrying about a bag going missing.

Snippets of My Year Away

Chasing the Blues

Blues here stands for turquoise seas and endless skies...
OK, are you ready to get to the heart of the joy of travel?

I'm going to share with you some moments of my amazing
gap year – 12 trips, 12 months, less than $12,000...you've
got to admit, that is pretty cool, and it was one of the
best times of my life! Make sure when you plan your trip
(whether one week, one month, or one year) that you
blog, write, or keep a journal. It is imperative to do this so
you can document and remember your experiences for a
lifetime, and share them with others.

Here are snippets from each trip. I hope they inspire you
to grab that passport and credit card, and hop on a plane
soon...

AUSTRALIA

It is no secret that the winter season is not my best friend,
so when the opportunity came about for me to travel
to Australia for a little while during our winter and their
summer, I quickly accepted the offer. Today marks my
6th day here, and overall it has been a very pleasing

experience. The weather, the people, and the unique animals are all beautiful. Before visiting, I never knew of the strong British culture that Australians have- reminds me a bit of being in London again!

-Aussies are fairly nice and they love American accents just as much as we love theirs
-This country is very expensive ($57 for a week bus pass, $10 for one hot dog, $20 dollars for a movie, etc.) BUT the minimum wage here is about $17 per hour.
-Netflix doesn't work here (so sad)

Currently I am in Sydney exploring each and everything this city has to offer which are amazing beaches, a beautiful aquarium, and tons of different restaurants.

FIJI

In one word, Fiji was absolutely AMAZING. This is a place I will have to visit again and stay longer. Nadi is literally filled with thousands of beautiful green trees and crystal blue water. The air feels totally different than the air anywhere else that I have ever been. The Fiji natives were probably some of the nicest people I have ever met. I spent my days in Fiji snorkeling, lying out on the beach, riding speed boats from island to island, and mixing and mingling with the natives. No trip to Fiji is complete without attending a Kava ceremony. Kava, is a local Fiji drink that is very popular among the locals. The taste is quite unique and is something you must experience while in Fiji.

Highlight of my trip: Being invited to a local's house for a traditional home cooked Fijian dinner.

BALI

After watching the movie "Eat, Pray, Love," I, like many other people, had a strong desire to visit Bali. While visiting Bali I wanted to experience the temples, the infamous Silent Retreat, and visit a medicine man.

I got to experience all of that and more. I spent one night in a silent retreat where the only rule was not to speak to anyone verbally. It was amazing. I prayed. I cried. I read books. I stared at the beautiful green trees. It was an experience I will never forget.

I also got the chance to visit the Monkey Temple, where hundreds of monkeys literally surround a religious temple. The monkeys are sacred, and while visiting the temple, you are in their territory and must respect them at all times. This is also a must do while in Bali.

If you are into massages and pampering, as I am, you will love Bali. I was able to go to a 4-star salon and get a 45-minute facial, 60-minute massage, manicure, and pedicure for a total price of $32 USD. That's right- 32 dollars. The prices were so low I was able to afford a massage every day of my journey.

Highlight of trip: Visiting the Silent Temple

THAILAND

I was very excited to visit the capital of Thailand as my introduction to the country. Bangkok, a very big, busy, and noisy city, had a lot to offer. From the night markets that sold everything from fruit to scorpions and maggots, to the abundance of massage parlors where you could get an hour Thai massage for less than $10 USD. Getting around the city was also pretty simple, I had the hotel where I stayed write down the address of the places I wanted to visit in Thai, so I could simply show the cab driver where I wanted to go. It helped with the language barrier and it made me feel a bit more comfortable traveling solo around the city.

Highlight of trip: Riding Elephants at the Samyook Elephant Camp

SOUTH AFRICA

Howzit!

It's Tuesday afternoon and I am currently en route to JFK Airport to board to flight to visit Cape Town, South Africa! Total travel time is 19 hours, can you believe it? That includes a 3 hour layover in Amsterdam!
I will be away for a total of 10 days (2 days will be spent on traveling).

Three South African Fun Facts:

1. South Africa is the second largest exporter of fruit in the world
2. South Africa has the cheapest electricity in the world
3. Three of the five fastest land animals live in South Africa – the cheetah (63 miles per hour), the wildebeest, and the lion.

MEXICO

Crystal blue water, handmade tortillas, and fun in the sun: Cabo San Lucas has so many different aspects that make for an incredibly beautiful city. I got the opportunity to visit Cabo for four days and three nights for less than $800.00. This price included a 4-star hotel, all-inclusive resort (food, alcoholic and non-alcoholic beverages) and a round-trip flight and shuttle to and from the airport. If you ever have an opportunity to snag an all-inclusive trip, take it! The money you save from not having to pay for breakfast, lunch, dinner, or drinks allows your spending money to go a long way. Here's what I spent my savings on, three activities you can't leave Cabo without experiencing:

1) Camel Riding & Outback Safari

This adventure takes you on a voyage far away from the tourist areas into the Baja peninsula. This excursion includes riding in a unique Mercedes Benz Unimog 4×4 trucks to explore a private, beachfront ranch, and also includes a guided nature walk where you walk and learn about the areas unique cactus and fauna. This excursion costs roughly $100 USD.

2) Swimming with Dolphins

I have had the chance to swim with dolphins in two other countries, but here in Cabo, I had the best experience. If you are a dolphin lover, as I am, you will enjoy the Dolphin Encounter. The price was a bit steep (about $180 USD), but it included 45 minutes of dolphin one-on-one play time, as well as an opportunity to swim with the beautiful mammals. This intimate excursion was sealed with a kiss from my dolphin, Sophie.

3) Sunset Cruises

Imagine the sun setting over a beautiful body of water. People all over came together on a 40-foot party boat to watch the sun dim, eat homemade tortillas, and enjoy complementary adult beverages. This cruise is a perfect way to meet other tourists and enjoy a relaxing view. For only about $50 USD, the next time you are in Cabo, you must experience this event. Only one word to describe it- amazing!

AMERICAN TRIPS TOO...

HAWAII

Relaxing. Sunny. Refreshing. Expensive. There are so many more words I could use to describe the beautiful island of Honolulu, HI. Honolulu is the state capital and the most populous city in the U.S. state of Hawaii. Situated on the island of Oahu, it is known worldwide as a major tourist destination; Honolulu is the main gateway to Hawaii and a major gateway into the United States of America.

For five days I had the opportunity to wake up to the sound of the ocean and smell the clean crisp air seep through the hotel room. Hawaii is definitely a place to go if you need to give yourself a break and simply relax. Of course, there are also many activities for the adventurous soul.

ATV riding, visiting the famous Polynesian Cultural Center, Dinner Cruises, and searching for the island's best food trucks are some of the activities you should have on your agenda.

During my visit to Honolulu, I stayed in the Waikiki area. Fortunately, having a car is not a huge necessity in this area. There are tons of shops, beaches, bars, and restaurants to choose from within walking distance of each other. If you do feel the urge to visit other places, tourism companies are happy to come get you from your hotel and take you away. But beware: the costs of this can surely increase by the day, but it is totally worth it to see as much of the island as possible.

If, by chance, you choose to sit on the beach and sip Mai-Tai's all week long and only choose to participate in one activity, it should definitely be the Polynesian Cultural Center. The Polynesian Cultural Center is a Polynesian-themed theme park located in Laie, on the northern shore of Oahu, Hawaii. Within eight simulated tropical villages, performers demonstrate various arts and crafts from throughout Polynesia. The place is absolutely breath-taking, and your trip to Hawaii would not be complete without a visit here.

I would recommend everyone plan to visit this beautiful place at some point in life. If you are a United States citizen, you don't even need a passport-but believe me when I say you will definitely feel like you are on a great escape.

Houston, TX

The people are nice, the food is better, and the shopping is fantastic! One of my dear college friends married her sweetheart in his hometown of Houston, TX, and I got to be a part of the wonderful festivities. For four days I got to explore this wonderful place, and it was quite enjoyable!

Anyone who knows me knows how much of a "foodie" I am! Eating has to be in my top three favorite things to do. While in Houston, I visited "The Breakfast Klub: The kofee shop that happens to serve great food" and boy are the right! (Yes! They interchange every letter 'c' with the letter 'k'.) I ordered tasty Chicken and Waffles and I couldn't have gotten a better seasoned dish. The atmosphere was amazing and the wait wasn't too long. My entire meal cost about $20. Not too bad! If you are ever in Houston, you must visit this place!

For lunch, I visited The Texas BBQ House. For this place I have one word: YUM!

San Antonio, TX - Must Explore: Downtown Riverwalk

If I had to describe San Antonio in one word it would be: GORGEOUS! I must admit that I would have never thought I would feel this way about San Antonio before my first visit, but boy am I glad to have been wrong. I lucked up and got to be in town the same week as the "Taste of San Antonio", an event that took place in the lovely River Walk area. The Taste is an event where people pay a set fee ($25 online and $30 in person) to taste different dishes at 12 different restaurants- what an amazing concept!!

ATLANTA

I was born and raised in the South (Florida), so it's only natural that I have a certain affinity for Southern states, and last weekend I had the opportunity to visit Atlanta, Georgia. I have visited Atlanta many times before, but this time I planned to do things differently; eat at new restaurants, visit new amusement places, and experience new nightlife.

The weather was beautiful and the entire city of Atlanta appeared to be in a really great mood and excited for the upcoming Labor Day weekend. The first stop for me was the Coca Cola Factory in downtown Atlanta. The Coca Cola Factory was very cute and exciting; I watched a short movie about how Coke products help improve people's lives, and afterward I was led into a room with Coke products from all over the world. Customers had the opportunity to drink as much of any Coke product that they desired, from countries throughout Europe and Latin America, it was amazing!

Later in the evening I dined at Rays on the River, and I must say it was some of the best seafood I have had in my entire life. The formal restaurant had free valet services and was actually set up right in front of a river, which gave it an amazing ambiance. I ordered the Seafood Platter, complete with crab cakes, salmon, shrimp, and scallops, as well as a glass of Moscato. I sat back and simply enjoyed the entire experience.

If you have never visited Atlanta, you must go! The friendly people, excellent nightlife, great shopping, and variety of activities make for an amazing time for anyone. I promise you won't have time to be bored at all! This city is also fairly inexpensive. I was able to stay at a fairly nice hotel and rent a car for three days for less than $300 (this cost was split with another person, for a grand total of $600).

I travel so much outside of the U.S., so to have the opportunity to explore a state in my own country and have so much fun was priceless.

Are you feeling fully inspired now? These diverse, amazing, and fun trips were enjoyed over the course of one fantastic year and in total cost me less than $12,000. (This included housing, flights, meals, souvenirs, tours, and more!)

Is it just me, or is that REALLY great value?

Time to start planning your travels now!

Pre-Travel Checklist

The day before you go on your trip, check again that you know where all of the following are and that you have them ready to hand:

Item	Check!
Passport	
Travel docs (pre-print boarding passes etc.)	
Visa documentation	
Travel insurance docs	
Hotel information	
Country or city guide book	
Any rental car documents	
Packed suitcase	

It is also a very good idea to have copies of your most important documents made and to leave them with a friend or family member, just in case.

In Case of Emergency

Hopefully no emergencies will arise at all, but it will give you peace of mind to know that if one does, you are well covered. Take note – a little prep before you leave could be your salvation, should a problem occur.

Store numbers of your emergency contacts – Not just on your cell phone, but also on paper, in case your phone is lost or breaks. Have your mom or dad, or best friend's number easily accessible in case you need it. Also, on your phone, store one of these numbers under the acronym ICE (in case of emergency), so that in a dire emergency, someone else will know who to call.

Ensure you have travel insurance sorted – Make sure you have all of the documents that you need, and have stashed copies with family in case you need them.

Always let someone know where you are – Whether you update social media or text a friend, leave a trail. Don't go wandering off into the desert/rainforest/Outback without telling another soul, just in case.

Keep emergency cash – Don't forget what I said about a crisp $100 bill being a very handy friend.

Learn the local equivalent of '911', wherever you go – always makes sense.

Stash It

What to Do With Your Belongings While Away

As you travel around the world, you may find that some environments are safer than others, especially when it comes to caring for your belongings.

The number one rule is to take good, trustworthy local advice on what to do with belongings. For example, the manager of your accommodations in Bali may strongly advise that you use the safe provided in your room – and you would do well to listen!

Here are a few things to bear in mind when it comes to looking after each of your precious belongings:

Looking After Your Cell Phone

There are a few things to bear in mind when you are trying to keep your cell phone safe:

1. Make sure you have a lock screen on it so that you need to use a code to access it. This makes it less attractive to thieves and could save you if it does fall into the wrong hands.

2. Be sure to insure it - You may not need to pay any extra money, it could be included on your main travel insurance, or some bank accounts offer insurance as a benefit for clients – just make sure you're covered.
3. Don't be flashy – Use your phone discreetly and don't rave about the latest version of, for example, an iPhone, in a country where it may be a rare and desirable item. You will only draw attention to yourself as a tourist, as well as potentially attract the wrong eyes to your phone.
4. Don't leave it unattended – sounds obvious, but I have seen phones left on bars at airports and in all kinds of other places. Always keep it with you – it is more than just a valuable item, it could be your best means of contact with the folks back home and the rest of the world.

Looking After Your Credit Cards

1. Don't carry them all in the same place – If you have five credit cards but keep them all in the same wallet, what happens if you lose that wallet? Always keep an emergency card separately from the rest, in the safe at your hotel.
2. Make sure you have the vital phone numbers relating to your cards stored safely – store the number that you will have to call if a card gets lost or stolen separately….it's no good just on the back of the card!
3. When in restaurants or other environments where you may use your card, never let the waiter or assistant process your credit card out of

sight. In some countries, there are scams where unscrupulous servers take copies of credit cards to use later, or process more money than you owe. Keep your eye on your card whenever it is used and always keep your receipts.

Looking After Your Rental Vehicle

1. Make sure that your paperwork is always in order and in the car– don't run the risk of getting in trouble if pulled over.
2. Don't drive your car in any rough areas of town. Not to scare you, but in some countries, car-jacking is relatively common and rental cars driven by clueless tourists will always be a target. Stick to the main areas of town, especially if driving alone.
3. Park in the right places – you don't want to have the hassle of paying fines or worse, being clamped or towed away. Read the signs and take more care than you might back at home.
4. Always keep a good level of gas in the car. You may try to get away with running on nearly empty at home, but trust me, spend a few extra dollars and make sure that you are never at risk of being stranded due to lack of fuel thousands of miles from home.

This is what the student travel advisors Gap 360 had to say on the subject of looking after your belongings:

"Keep your valuables in a bag that has straps long enough to allow you to carry it across your body. This makes it harder for thieves to snatch your bag from you. If you plan to carry your valuables in a daypack, then wear it on your front. You may think it makes you look like a geek, but that's a small price to pay for being able to keep an eye on your gap year kit and will help prevent someone from raiding your pockets or unexpectedly slashing open your bag. As an extra precaution you can buy a bag that has two zips, which can then be secured together with a padlock."

When traveling on some buses it's normal for your main bag or backpack to be tied to the roof. This is generally safe. However, it is best to watch your bag being placed onto the roof, and then jump off the bus quickly once you've reached your destination to ensure you retrieve it quickly. Please note that you should not leave any valuables in this bag, especially not in any of the side pockets. You never know when an opportunist thief may try their luck when you're not looking. You can purchase sacks that cover your whole bag, helping disguise it, and preventing thieves from having a quick rummage through it. It also has the added bonus of keeping your bag clean and dry."

This is all great advice, and as long as you always apply a hefty dose of common sense, you have the best chance of keeping all your belongings safe from theft or loss.

Guide to Volunteering Abroad

It is an exceptionally special thing to volunteer - particularly abroad. Helping other people just like you, but also so different from you, possibly on the other side of the world for no monetary gain….it can be one of life's most rewarding gifts.

It takes some planning though. Before you decide to set off for your nearest African village, ask yourself a few key questions:

1) How long should I go for?

You need to think about this one carefully. Your time away may be dictated by your normal study or work schedule back home, or the amount of savings you have, for example. Can you manage a whole summer? How long can you afford not to work? There will definitely be something that suits you exactly – you just have to find it!

2) Where should I go?

Pick a continent, any continent. There are volunteering projects practically everywhere. Rather than be overwhelmed by the choices, you need to think hard about the sort of places in which you would like to volunteer.

Aid projects vary from country to country, and town to town. Do you think you want to help with disaster relief, or work on slowly building up a disadvantaged community? Research the relevant NGOs and organizations where you can join an established program. Then, wherever in the world you choose, you need to make sure you have both the airfare and commitment.

3) What kind of volunteer can I be?

Think about any special skills you might have. Are you a nurse, do you speak multiple languages, are you a teacher, or in another type of helpful professional? You need to field your key skills, and are also likely to have to undergo a little initial training, however experienced you may be. You are added real value by sharing your skills, so be proud and don't be shy about letting everyone know how you can help.

Teachers can teach English to children in need, or business people from English-speaking countries could help teach adults, so that their job opportunities are expanded. Experienced builders are vital, and can oversee building wells, hospitals, and schools, for example. Sharing your skills with underprivileged communities is an excellent thing to do.

4) Paid placement or not?

If you pay a fee to an organization, it normally means there will be accommodations provided, food, and an English-speaking contact. A portion of your fee is usually donated to the charity or project, but the downside is that it can be a bit pricey. Some organizations don't charge at all, but these tend to be more obscure. One good option is to raise your own funds and then to volunteer abroad, so you cut costs but cover all expenses.

5) Which projects?

There are SO many to choose from, but choose wisely. Take a good look at the company's website, blogs, and social media pages to learn more. Compile a long list, and then consider the projects for which you could be the most helpful, and which will ultimately do the most good, in your eyes.

However, when it comes to volunteering, you have to go with your gut, rather than a score out of ten, to a certain extent. Once you have totally fallen in love with a project, really go for it!

6) Time to Apply

When you apply, don't hold back. Let them know exactly how fabulous and committed you really are. If you have relevant experience, humbly shout about it. If you have volunteered before, modestly tell them the works. The best volunteering programs field thousands of applications, so let the project coordinators know exactly how special you are!

Dealing With Culture Shock

Traveling abroad for any reason, whether it is for vacation or educational purposes, can come with a lot of culture shock. Culture shock, as defined by the Webster Dictionary, is "the sudden exposure to an unfamiliar culture: the feelings of confusion and anxiety experienced by somebody suddenly encountering an unfamiliar cultural environment."

You can experience culture shock as quickly as on the plane ride to another country, or a week into your trip after arriving in the country. It is different for many people.

As for me, I have experienced culture shock in many of the countries I have traveled such as India, South Africa, and Thailand. While visiting Thailand, I was approached by a few locals who were dying to touch my skin and my hair! One person had explained in his broken English that they had never seen an African American woman in real life, and they were simply amused at my presence. In India I often dealt with stares from many people as I traveled throughout the town-it made me quite uncomfortable! But there is good news! The feeling of culture shock usually doesn't last for very long. Once you get used to the stares and the finger pointing, you realize that most of the time people are just genuinely interested in who you are and where you came from; most of the time they would love to practice their English with you and learn about the place you come from. Many of them even offer to show you around their country. Culture shock is normal, and isn't something that lasts for too long. Here are some tips that I use to help me deal with it:

1. I research the country thoroughly before traveling so that I can get a sense of the culture norms. Example: What do women usually wear in a particular country? Is spitting on the ground customary, or a big no-no? Is the country diverse at all?
2. Understand that in some places, there may be people who have never seen a person who looks like you before in real life. Imagine how you would react if the shoe were on the other foot. Most of the time the stares and points from people are harmless!
3. I befriend a local or an expat who can help me maneuver the new place I am visiting/living.
4. I blog or journal about my experiences. Sometimes after getting a little frustrated, writing helps calm me down and puts me in a comfortable frame of mind.

The bottom line is that culture shock is real and very common, but it is nothing that anyone can't get through! Keep an open mind and you will be sure to bounce right back to the same mind frame you had before your visit.

Discount Travel Websites

I am often asked which websites I use the most to secure low budget travel. Below I have listed the top seven sites I use the most. Keep in mind that often to find the best deal, I must play around with different dates, departure locations, and websites. In some cases I've found that I could save as much as $450 on a roundtrip flight if I left from an airport an hour or two away from home. This is definitely a bargain! In other cases I have found that if I leave a day or two after my desired departure date, I can save as much as $150!

My advice: take an hour or two and search, search, search! It can save you hundreds of dollars!

1. www.cheapoair.com
2. www.cheaptickets.com
3. www.southwest.com
4. www.airfarewatchdog.com
5. www.hotels.com
6. www.priceline.com
7. www.theflightdeal.com

Having fun at the Taj Mahal in India.

Enjoying the cultural festivities   Kissing Koalas in Melbourne, Australia
in Bangkok, Thailand.

In awe of the Sydney Opera House

Visiting temples in Seoul, South Korea

Before riding the Beautiful London Eye!

Water Zip lining in Cabo San Lucas, Mexico

Feeling on top of the world in Athens, Greece

Spectacular Mountain views in Honolulu, Hawaii

The architecture in Downtown Rome, Italy is amazing!

Ready To Go:

Congratulations, YBP! You've taken the first step and completed reading this book. Hopefully it's gotten your creative juices flowing. I hope by now you are inspired, motivated, and ready to go!

Take a moment to fill out the questionnaire below, which will help you plan your trip(s).

List your top three must visit places soon:

1) _____
2) _____
3) _____

When do you plan on visiting these places?
1) _____
2) _____
3) _____

Will you travel alone or with people?

_____

What is your TOTAL budget for your trip(s)?
1) _____
2) _____
3) _____

List three hostels/hotels that are in your budget in the area of your dream trip(s). (Remember to sign up for rewards programs to help collect free nights and discounts)

1) _____
2) _____
3) _____

List any excursions, activities, etc. you want to participate in on your trip(s).

1) _____
2) _____
3) _____

What tourist attractions/activities do you plan to visit or take part in?

1) _____
2) _____
3) _____

What NON tourist attractions do you plan to visit or take part in?

1) _____
2) _____
3) _____

How do you plan to save and budget to visit these places?

_____

_____

_____

_____

When is your deadline for saving and planning your trip(s)?

_____

_____

Now take a look at this discount website and find the best deal- don't forget that sometimes bundling your flight, hotel, and rental car may make a better deal. http://www.kiplinger.com/article/spending/T059-C000-S001-23-best-travel-sites-to-save-you-money.html

Good Luck! You now have all that you need to plan your amazing trip on a budget.